For What It's
Worth

*The Downward Spiral Of
The Church Into The World*

KENNETH LEWIS THD

Ark House Press
arkhousepress.com

© 2023 Kenneth Lewis ThD

All rights reserved. Apart from any fair dealing for the purpose of study, research, criticism, or review, as permitted under the Copyright Act, no part may be reproduced by any process without written permission.

Unless otherwise stated scripture quotations from The Authorized (King James) Version. Rights in the Authorized Version in the United Kingdom are vested in the Crown. Reproduced by permission of the Crown's patentee, Cambridge University Press.

Cataloguing in Publication Data:
Title: For What It's Worth
ISBN: 978-0-6456366-6-6 (pbk)
Subjects: Church; Christian Living;

Design by initiateagency.com

Is the church heading into apostasy? Why is the church sowing wild oats? We are seeing her rapidly going down the path of wallowing in the worlds culture and adopting the ways of a sinful world. This is being done by many evangelical churches and also those who are independent churches who do not identify as evangelical but who are conservative theologically. Let's delve into some thoughts on this downfall and the remedy. Then let's talk about how we can get back on the right path?

This book is dedicated to: My dear wife Theresa Lewis

She has been my rock and help-meet keeping me focused and on track. She is my spiritual partner through deep waters as well as those prosperous times and never fails to have a kind and sweet word to anyone who needs encouragement. Her life has been given to the reading and understanding of God's Word and prayer and her example to me has been exemplary, leading me to a greater depth of spiritual growth through Christ Jesus and His Word. I have been enriched throughout our years together and thank God for every moment He has given me with her.

Contents

Introduction ix

PART I: BRINGING THE WORLD INTO THE CHURCH.

Chapter 1: Adapting to the Culture of An Unsaved World! 5
    CLUE ONE: Rock And Roll Music 6
    CLUE TWO: Band Led Services 9
    CLUE THREE: Feminism and Wrongful Leadership 12
Chapter 2: Twisting the Great Commandment 21
    CLUE FOUR: Emphasis On Love While Compromising On Sin. 22
Chapter 3: Subverting God's Teaching On Justice 26
    CLUE FIVE: Emphasis on Social Justice – Not the Gospel 28

PART II: THE CHURCHES SLIDE INTO COMPROMISE

Chapter 4: The Christian School Domino Effect 33
    CLUE SIX: Little Preaching on Repentance 35
    CLUE SEVEN: An Emphasis on Money 37
    CLUE EIGHT: Not Believing Genesis One 38

Part III: The Road Upward – Returning to Righteousness in Your Church

RESTORE POINT 1: Repentance – as a church or an individual, renew your relationship with God. 43
RESTORE POINT 2: Righteousness – put on the new man and walk in holiness. 44
RESTORE POINT 3: Prune – getting rid of dead sinful and unholy branches in your church body and practices. 45
RESTORE POINT 4: Salt and Light – you should be an irritant as well as light in your community! 47

Epilogue/Conclusion 51
Bibliography 53
References 55
Acknowledgments 57
About the Author 59

Introduction

I wrote this book because I am deeply concerned about the church's downward push into the culture of this world. I have observed the church for over 60 years, and it is difficult to watch what is happening today. I find that very few pastors are preaching about it. Instead many seem to be encouraging this as a means to building their church through making it more palatable to the world. It is a slide toward apostasy which we know is coming because the Scripture warns us of it. (2Thessalonians 2:3 HCSB *Don't let anyone deceive you in any way. For that day will not come unless the apostasy comes first...*) However, watching it happen causes me to sound the alarm to try to warn people about the problems with these evil tactics and gimmicks.

I am not simply referring to the liberal churches that are mostly mainstream denominations today. I am also talking about the so-called evangelical churches, many of the mega-churches, conservative denominations and those who hold to the fundamentals of the faith. Those whose theology is true to the Word of God, at least to the best of their thinking. Those who believe in salvation by grace through faith in Christ without works.

I must confess, I do not feel comfortable in the average church today. It is like going to something foreign. I do not enjoy it. I do not sense the Spirit of God there, at least in most services. I have talked with people who say they cannot find a good church home anymore. It is difficult because the modern church is so different and may I say, worldly?

Let's define the word: "Worldly" refers to that which pertains to Satan's world which is not holy nor Christ-like.

Having a solid background in approaching this subject over many years, though not considering myself an expert, however, preaching over 150 revivals, teaching private Christian school, directing choirs, being a soloist on many stages, having recorded, preached and sang in many churches across this country I am now just an old warrior of the faith with a passion for truth.

As an octogenarian, I still feel like a young man. The mind stays young and does not seem to grow old, but the body is a whole different issue. I still think I can do many things until I try to do them and then I realize I am really getting old. But don't get me wrong nor misunderstand me. I am very young at heart and so are most true believers of my age group. It is very easy for us to see the major changes throughout the years from our vantage point and it is alarming.

So, I wanted to do something else meaningful while I still had time and write this book and say what I thought needed to be said. You can take it or leave it. But my hope is that it causes you to evaluate the progressive direction the church is taking because the work of Christ is too important to take casually.

Please read this book through to the end. Parts of it may upset you because you are younger and raised in a different church atmosphere. But hear me out and listen to the Spirit of God as you read and honestly allow God to work.

Take note of what is called Christian today. You will have to agree much of it is sad. People claiming the name of Christ who think killing babies is fine. People who indulge in Scripturally known sins and excuse it are numerous. Women pastors (Saddleback to name one), lesbian pastors, same-sex weddings in churches, the acceptance of Sodom and Gomorrah is a very telling downfall into the pits of theological Hell itself. It shows Satan's hold over much of Christendom today.

The Church must stay holy. It must be pure without spot or wrinkle. We must work to reject all impurities which might be considered a blight on the precious Name of Jesus Christ in our church body. Our clothing, our music, our speech, our behaviors and all that we say and do must reflect a Holy God. We must work hard to achieve a high grade in that category. We must be the opposite of an immoral world, not in lock-step with it! We should be rejected by the world, not accepted. We should be hated at times, like Jesus was, love like Jesus loved, while bearing our cross courageously no matter what the cost.

If you have not looked around lately, the world is rejecting Christianity en masse, that is, true Biblical Christianity. America upholds Muslims and criticizes Christians. I never thought I would see the day this could happen in America, but we are living in it. The world does not like what we stand for or against. They do not want purity and holiness which limits their immoral activities and to them it creates agitation.

Everything is upside down in our society. They want to reduce our police forces while allowing rioters to burn down our cities in the name of social justice. They want the right to kill innocent babies they do not want and it has become a pagan ritual. Take for example the uproar that ensued from the decision of the US Supreme Court on striking down Roe vs Wade. We were horrified when we read in the Old Testament about how the Israelites would throw their babies into a burning fire to worship a false god by the name of Molech. Now we hear that they harvest baby parts to sell on the black market and can do little to stop it. However, on the contrary, our judiciary puts people in jail that expose it.

The natural world wants to indulge in unnatural sex. Kids are told to pick their own gender no matter what their birth sex is. Americans, including many Christians voted for a president who said that children as young as eight should be allowed to choose their gender.[1] It is a sad day in America when one of our leaders takes this position against God's standards in creation. I understand! People get used to things, compromise, and holiness slips down the drain.

Teens are confused about who they are. Parents are shocked when their teenagers come home from school and say they think they are a boy when they were born a girl. Many of our parents fail at teaching their children the moral behaviors of the Scriptures. Many are too busy being a buddy or friend or trying to be cool with their child while failing to show them the fullness of God's Word while they were growing up and developing. All these things are from a breakdown in the family.

Much of the church is on shaky ground today and heading toward apostasy rapidly. We seem to be more interested in entertaining people so they will come to our services then we are in preaching repentance and purity. It is true that we would have fewer people if we preached all of the Word of God, but the result would be that our churches would be pure and holy and powerful.

I trust this book will open your eyes to some of the clues that are leading us down the road to apostasy and give you some ideas on how we can get back on the right path.

PART I

Bringing The World Into The Church.

For some time now, we have been trying to impress the world with our Christianity. We have sought to make our churches palatable to the average person on the street so they will be more accepting of our beliefs in Jesus. Somehow, somewhere, we began to believe that we had to attract people to our services, make them feel comfortable by dressing down to a street level, trying to sing God's praise with a pop music flair so people would know that we are hip and not weird or strange. Then the world might accept our Jesus or at least listen to our message about Him.

When Paul said *To the weak became I as weak, that I might gain the weak: I am made all things to all men, that I might by all means save some* (I Corinthians 9:22) he did not mean to adopt the ways and mentality of a sinful world.

Evidently some in the church have felt that Christ was not enough to draw people to Himself when He explicitly said: *And I, if I be lifted up from the earth, will draw all men unto me (myself).* (John 12:32) Does Messiah need us to adopt worldly measures to bring people to Him? Contrary to our humanly-absorbed thinking, absolutely not! It is a spiritual issue. It takes prayer and fasting, holiness and purity on our part so that when we ask God for souls, we will reap a harvest that is genuine, not superficial.

When I was a kid growing up in a Baptist church, things were fairly strict. When I was about two years old, my mother had come to know Christ as her Savior and began a journey with our Lord. My father was in the Army and shipped overseas at that time. He served during World War II. He did not know Christ as his Savior at that point.

When my father came back from the war, my mother took him to church, and he came to Christ and began his walk with our Lord. Eventually he became a deacon and served in that capacity the rest of his life.

PART I: Bringing The World Into The Church.

My brother and I went forward in church one Sunday night and received Christ as our Savior and we began our journey with Him. I was only six years old and he was nine. I was not baptized until I was nine years old.

At six years of age I surrendered to Christ and I remember that event well. We went to all the services, revival meetings, whatever and whenever possible and became an integral part of that church that grew from a small church to well over 500 people. I carried Gospel tracts and a New Testament in my pocket to elementary school and pointed many of my classmates to Christ and brought them to church.

We did not attend the theaters. Nobody told us not to go. The preacher did not preach about it. We just knew it was not for us as believers to be there. When I got to Junior High, I did not attend the dances. I did not want to. My parents did not tell me not to go. I knew in my heart that it was not for me. I never went to prom and never attended any dances. I have no regrets! They were not the crowd I wanted to associate with as a believer.

You may think that we were super strict, but I can tell you that none of my large youth group went to prom but one girl. We just did not go because we felt it was part of the culture of the world and we did not want to be part of that.

Compare my situation in that church then to churches today and you will find that things are much different. Girls wear their prom dresses to Sunday morning church following prom night at school, many with their strapless gowns and think nothing of it. They want people to know that they went to prom. Christians attend the theater and preachers talk openly about the movies from the pulpit, using illustrations from them.

I ask you, "What has changed?" Did God change? Are the proms more modest now than they were then? Are the movies purer and more moral in their scenes than they used to be? I believe the answer to those questions is an emphatic NO. Prom dresses are skimpier than they used to be, and movies are full of sex and anti-Christian living.

So I believe that believers slow creep into the world has led the church to slowly creep into the culture of the world and that leads to apostasy, false teachings, acceptance of immoral living, immature Christians, and many false or fake Christians. Some make it through with beliefs intact but many fall by the wayside. It reminds me of Israel in the Old Testament where they continually sought the gods of the heathen world and neglected Jehovah and their covenant with Him.

There are many clues to this drift into apostasy. Some of which I want to address in this book. You may take issue with me on some of these, but I simply ask you to read them, pray about them, and decide for yourself where you stand. Some of which we can leave to Romans 14 issues.

Chapter One

Adapting to the Culture of An Unsaved World!

Jude 1:4 *I say this because some ungodly people have wormed their way into your churches, saying that God's marvelous grace allows us to live immoral lives.* NLT

When we look at the world around us, we must notice that many of their ideas on morality are foreign to the Word of God. Yes, there is good in the world. That comes from the innate conscience that God has embedded in each person when they were created. He gave them some abilities to discern good and evil, to choose right and to dislike wrong.

However, man was born with a sinful heart and that heart (or soul) is prone to do wrong and that is very evident in our society. With some people, it begins at an early age. With others it may take much longer and with others, they keep it tamed throughout most of their life and try to do good. But God says that the heart of man is deceitful and desperately wicked.

This world is ruled by Satan. If you are new to the faith and do not know this, it is New Testament Theology 101. God is ultimately over all, but for now, Satan is the "prince of the power of the air" and runs to and fro throughout the earth seeking whom he may devour. He prowls about like a lion trying to deceive. He has his hordes of multiple millions of demons (fallen angels that were kicked out of heaven), infiltrating our homes and churches and causing chaos in this world, possessing many and causing many to be in distress.

Satan hates God and Satan is the god of this world and the culture of this world is ruled by Satan. So, when a Christian adapts to the culture of this world, he is walking in dangerous territory spiritually. Much of it seems innocent, but it is a slow decline and most people do not know they are sliding downward until they hit the bottom.

Also, when the Christians in the Church begin adapting it to the world, the church begins to lose its power. When God is not in complete control of the church and as the church grabs more and more of the world's culture, the church becomes an instrument of the world instead of a holy and righteous, separated and sanctified body for the glory of its founder the Lord of Lords and King of Kings.

There are some clues to this decline into apostasy that I would like to present.

CLUE ONE: Rock And Roll Music

Rock and Roll music came in the late 1950's, mainly with Elvis Presley, Bill Haley and the Comets, Jerry Lee Lewis and others. I clearly remember those days because I was a teenager, having graduated from High School in June of 1960.

Before that time, I listened to show tunes and love songs on my "AM only" home or car radio. I was one of the fortunate kids since my dad was in the car business. I had a car to drive to school since age 14 and there were no others in my Jr High school that had their own car. In fact, in high school, there were very few who owned a car and drove to school and the school was quite large.

But I had a nice custom rod to drive and I loved music. I was in Madrigals at our large high school of about 2,300 kids and was in a quartet at church as well as choir and did solo work. Music was my life. And I disliked rock and roll when it came on the radio in my car and displaced the beautiful music I had been used to, so I would turn it off. Pat Boone, The Fontaine Sisters, Julius LaRosa, The Four Lads, The Four Freshman and many many others donned my radio frequency. To me, rock and roll just was not very good music. It was not classy and seemed like cheap music with too much beat and terrible singers that had no quality in their voices, with the exception of Elvis and a few others.

Rock and roll music comes with the terrible connotation or derivation from sexual immorality. It was called rock and roll because it illustrated what a car does when two people are in the back seat having sex. Its beat included loud drums, loud guitars and fast rhythms, some syncopated music with an off-beat and originated from an immoral undertone. Why do we want to bring that into the church?

At church, when missionaries would show films of their work in Africa, you would see the men and women dancing to beating drums and sensual music (music? so called). The witch doctor was there and most of the time the dancing and drums were trying to conjure up some demonic activity. Demon possession was very common throughout the tribes and villages of Africa at that time. Now, dancing and music seem to resemble much of that culture which was inspired from the pits of Hell. Much of which had and has demonic activity associated with it. Many rock and roll artists today speak of using a spirit guide and channeling help from spirits.

Bringing such music into the church established by Jesus Christ, that is to be holy and pure, is an insult. Do we think that such hard drums and loud guitars played in fast rhythms will get the people excited about a holy God? Do we have to gen-up emotions and feelings to get people excited about their Savior or is it just pandering to our fleshly appetites to conjure up some sort of false spiritual emotion that looks spiritual. I believe strongly in the latter.

Rock and roll music is out of place in the church of Jesus Christ.

Let me digress a moment. Much of the new music used in our churches today is not rock and roll. There is much that is good and that I personally enjoy. However, there is much that is pathetic. Much of which is theologically flawed, too repetitious, on the spiritual level of a kindergartner, and for much of it, just plain offensive.

I could give you example after example, but that is not my desire in writing this book. That should be the worship leaders' job and the pastors to scrutinize and make sure we are nourishing the flock with wholesome, theologically correct, Christ-honoring music that was not written by a twenty-something year old who knows nothing about the foundational doctrines of the Scriptures. I am shocked at pastors who allow such doctrinally unsound music to be sung by their worship teams. What is the desire in allowing such music? Carnality? Pride? Losing touch with a holy God? Perhaps repentance is in order for many pastors who are feeding such trash to their churches in hopes of looking up-to-date and cool.

Let me state this emphatically: Music is NOT worship!!! We falsely call music directors Worship leaders. What is worship? Without going into a long dissertation on the subject, let me say briefly that Worship is exalting the worth-ship of our Lord. It seeks to praise and honor His Name. It is done with one's heart in speaking, reading poetry, music and mostly alone in our closet. It comes from a loving heart that seeks to honor the Lord

Jesus in our walk and talk. It is not in a crowd crooning words and raising hands altogether in a song while swaying and dancing to the beat as if one is at a rock concert celebrating the vibe.

Music is critical to the health of our churches! What passes for music in many of our churches today is, in my opinion, sad. Churches should put together better music services, but even with a highly paid staff, many seem to suffer. I will cover more on this issue in the next segment.

CLUE TWO: Band Led Services

When you sit in the pews or chairs of most modern churches, there are no hymn books, no pianos, and no organs, no choirs, no music directors, but there are some men, usually dressed in Levi's, and casually dressed women up front with their microphones and instruments whaling away on some semi-loud rhythmic song with not much spiritual content. There are one to three huge screens hanging high up front with words on them so everybody can sing the songs in unison while following the bands leading.

The music we use in our churches to honor and worship our great and powerful, holy and righteous Lord Jesus Christ is dreadfully lacking. Much of it is a disgrace to His holy Name! My heart is saddened by the lack of decorum we have for our precious Lord in seeking to worship and honor Him.

Now, I must say that I like much of the newer music and I must also tell you that I tire of some of the older hymns, just like many of you. For example, "When the Roll is Called Up Yonder" is one I find tiring. Also, "He Lives." The words are good, but the melody needs a lot of updating. So, please do not misunderstand me. I have played guitar (not well) since I was 14 years old. There is nothing I love more than the sound of a lone guitar finger-picking out a beautiful tune.

What I think is disgraceful is the lack of politeness and honorable work with which we honor our King. The trite phrases we use in our music. The poor tune's that have no real melody. The lack of sound Scriptural theology used in our music. We do not sing parts anymore because most of the music written today has none written and no one has a music sheet with which to sing a part and the bands do not play enough of a full sound or score in music to follow it with a part. I know, I have tried to sing a bass with some of the music and it is difficult unless you only harmonize. Sometimes I can sing an alto part or a tenor part which I do.

What would be preferable would be a small orchestra or regular band like a high school band. I have seen it done in some churches and it is beautiful. Instead we use a typical "dance band" style. I attended a church that ran 3,000 people that was band led. It had a huge platform with large side platforms that would accommodate an orchestra and a choir. I thought, how wonderful that would be. When I asked the Worship Leader about it, he said that he could not get people to commit to doing all the services each time and each week, which I find saddens me.

The mere size of that church would have had so much talent you could have had several orchestras and choirs. But Christians evidently do not want to give of their time and talent to provide an awesome worship experience to praise and honor the King and on the other hand, many Worship leaders are not talented enough to direct an orchestra. So, we hobble along with a 6- or 8-piece dance band playing guitars and drums. What a sad effort given to honor our King!

Can you see evidence of a downward drift in the New Testament Church? It is not just the preachers that seem to be drifting downward, it is also the people pulling churches down.

When I grew up in our church of a few hundred, people played their instruments for the evening service and now we do not even have evening services because people do not want to be bothered and I think, perhaps, preachers do not want to preach them. My first pastorate I preached in a small church, running just under a hundred people, in a rural community. I preached Sunday morning, Sunday afternoon at the rest home, Sunday evening service and Wednesday evening prayer meeting service. Three new messages a week because I used my Sunday morning message to preach at the rest home. Today, preachers preach one message a week in the average church and think they are doing well.

Churches need to get together and work hard to put on the best music program they can on Sunday mornings. We need to quit trying to attract the world into our services and begin encouraging believers who come to the services. That is why we gather! Right!?! The church is a gathering for believers, not sinners. We are to go out into the highways and hedges, the workplaces and neighbors and share Jesus. The gathering on Sunday is for believers to worship their King and be encouraged and uplifted by a great teaching message from God's Word and to sing songs and hymns together.

We need to grab all the talent we can get from our church and find someone who knows music well enough to lead a small orchestra, at least some horns and strings. It will grow. You generally will not be playing rock and roll in an orchestra, but the music will be fuller and richer with the instruments. Put the guitars and drums with the horns and make a joyful sound to the Lord. Honor Him with all you can. Work hard for your King! Let's stop and assess the need and put people to work. You have many people who quit playing instruments when they left high school and they need to be activated for service again to play for the Lord.

At first, it will be slow recruiting people, but it will grow over time. Had we been asking people to serve in an orchestra for 20 or so years, we would now have an abundance of talent to fill the need. But so many churches began to follow the world and its allurement of rock and roll music and opted to put together a small band and have lost the essence of true worship. We have gone down the path leading to apostasy by following the culture of a world full of lost and dying sinful men. The church has been losing its purity in so doing and has been tainting herself with worldliness.

CLUE THREE: Feminism and Wrongful Leadership

God created three institutions: The Home, The Government and The Church. They all fall under the same Biblical guidelines. Many will seek to take issue on this point, however, let me explain why I believe it to be so. God created the world and everything in it through the Lord Jesus Christ. God is the same yesterday, today and forever. He does not change. Do you think He has a different standard for the Home than for the Church? Do you think He has a different standard for the Home and Church than He does for Government? Of course not! His standards are unchangeable. If you look at His standards for these institutions, you will see they are all the same, Only the people in positions of leadership change and duties are different, but His standards for the roles of men and women do not and did not change.

In the Old Testament, there were kings that led Israel, not queens. There were male priests in the Temple, not women priests. Leadership was always male. Adam was first formed than Eve to be his companion but taken out of the body of the man. I did not make this up! It was God's way from the beginning. *"For Adam was first formed then Eve"* I Timothy 2:13

I have no axe to grind. When I traveled across the country, or pastored a church, many times I thought my wife could do a better job than myself in teaching or preaching, but I knew it was my responsibility from God to do it. So, I did my job with joy.

If we do not follow God's leadership in the institutions we oversee, who will? We have left the leadership to those who were willing to work and not followed the Scriptures. I believe men have been very guilty in leadership at home and at church.

In the Church. We have strayed far from the Scriptures and traditions passed down through the centuries. The Scripture is clear about the Church being led by men. That is not to say that women are not capable because many are and many surpass the men in skills by far who are available for the task, but God gave the admonition for men to lead the church.

Men are to be the preachers, elders, deacons, and women are not to be leaders over the male population of the church. Women are to teach other women, especially younger women on how to be godly, but our churches have traveled far away from the Scriptural teachings given to the Church.

Look at what the Scripture says in I Corinthians 14:34-35 about the role of women in the Church: *(1Co 14:34) Let your women keep silence in the churches: for it is not permitted unto them to speak; but they are commanded to be under obedience, as also saith the law.*

(1Co 14:35) And if they will learn any thing, let them ask their husbands at home: for it is a shame for women to speak in the church.

Do not try to theorize that this was just the custom in Paul's day like some weak-kneed preachers have tried to say. Some teachers compromise Scripture because they are afraid of what the culture might think. Stand up! Be true to the Scripture without excuses!

Albert Barnes in his commentary states: *These things constituted the business of the public teaching; and in this the female part of the congregation were to be silent. "They were not to teach the people, nor were they to interrupt those who were speaking"* [3]

Paul reiterates this in I Timothy 2:11-13. *Let the woman learn in silence with all subjection. But I suffer not a woman to teach, nor to usurp authority over the man, but to be in silence. For Adam was first formed, then Eve.*

Again, it is very clear if you believe Scripture. Paul does not change this for different circumstances. This is God's way of doing Church meetings.

In Titus 2:3-5, Paul makes clear that the older, more mature spiritually, should teach the younger women. That would carry over to older women who are new converts. They should be taught by older women believers.

(Verse 3) The aged women likewise, that they be in behavior as becomes holiness, not false accusers, not given to much wine, teachers of good things; (4) That they may teach the young women to be sober, to love their husbands, to love their children, (5) To be discreet, chaste, keepers at home, good, obedient to their own husbands, that the word of God be not blasphemed.

One more point that I want to stress in I Timothy 3:12 *Let the deacons be the husbands of one wife, ruling their children and their own houses well.* Women are not to hold the office of Pastor or Overseer or a deacon. Women are not to hold any office in the church that would be classified as Scriptural leadership or an office that puts them over men.

I would like to expand this thought a little further. Women should not be secretaries or assistants to pastors or deacons. There have been many pastors and deacons who have fallen prey to temptation over having a female working with them every day. Pastors, you should have male secretaries and assistants. Call them what you want but this would prevent leaders from such close association with a female helper. Now, let me say that women can handle these tasks as well as any man or even better, but we must protect these leaders from being the next story on the television news program and avoiding a black eye being placed publicly on the church. Too often we have seen the dirty laundry of some church being hung out to a hateful world who is looking for anything to criticize and demean a church's testimony.

It is the same principle of deciding things within the church rather than going to the courts and publicly airing differences. Hanging out our so-called dirty laundry publicly just reinforces the worlds' belief that they knew all along that there was nothing different in the people of the church or its adherents. That church people are hypocrites and phony. Paul asks the question... "Why?"

I may be treading on controversial ground, but just because the culture scoffs at what God says in His word does not mean we are not to obey it. And just because preachers are afraid to preach against the cultural social norms does not mean it does not apply to the church and is not right and correct.

In our churches today we have so many who are afraid to speak the truth. I will cover this subject more in a later chapter. But let me continue the subject concerning our wonderful and lovely females that are such an integral part of our churches.

Years ago, when I was traveling and doing revival meetings, a man came up to me after the service to complain. In that day, we traveled with about twenty-five plus people around the country, singers, sound crew, secretaries, children's workers, family teacher, youth worker, etc and many of the singers were young women in their twenties and attractive. Their clothes were modest, and they all wore the same outfits because we ordered them for the gals and guys.

But this man was complaining because he was taken with the beauty of one of the girls and it bothered him with lust. Obviously, we might assume that he had a spiritual issue. My point is this: Women in front leading can cause men to lust. You may say, "That's their problem!" That is true but perhaps that is why God gave us these special instructions for the church.

Women can influence men by the way they dress or the way they sway and move or dance to the rhythm of the music.

In the Old Testament, I believe they had all male choirs in the synagogue or temple. I think in our churches our choirs ought to wear robes to conceal women's bodies because of the effect they can have on various men. You may scoff at that idea of modesty, but in our society that is filled with such immodesty, our women ought to, at least, think of modesty in the church.

Perhaps, we ought to opt for all male worship teams, or better yet, let's be led by a male music leader and a choir wearing robes while using these newer music books that have many of the great hymns of the faith as well as many new songs that are wonderful to sing.

I am not stating that women ought not sing in the church but as I stated in an earlier section, I believe there ought to be women soloists, trios, instrumentalists, etc. Using their talents for the Lord is wonderful and useful for His glory while dressing modestly.

We must be careful to follow Scriptural teachings as closely as we can. Men as well as women should dress modestly and appropriately before the church. Women are not to be in leadership roles over men in the church is very clear from God's Word.

Sometimes, I think we Christians are the most simple-minded of all peoples because we let our guard down while putting ourselves in compromising situations over and over again. It is just the grace of God that more men in the ministry have not fallen from grace in their churches. We only know about the ones that make the headlines in the newspapers as Satan spreads the shamefulness of Christian immorality to the whole world to embarrass the church and God's people. May God help us!

In the home. The home is a very sacred place to God, and He gave us some strict commandments that should be kept responsibly. However, many of our Christian homes are far from following Scriptural mandates and have become part of this world's culture of unholiness and a sham.

In my estimation, too many Christian homes go to church on Sunday, if at all, and live in the context of the world the other six and one-half days. It is about doing your duty for an hour and then going about what you like the rest of the week.

The weakest part of most homes are the dads. Many refuse to dedicate their lives in service to the Lord in their home. Instead, they let the women take the lead spiritually and they simply follow. That is totally backwards from Scripture and a recipe for mediocrity.

Men are to be the leaders in the home. That is their role. They are to be the spiritual leaders. They are to take the yoke and lead the family the way God leads them. Ephesians 5 gives us the outline for it among other passages but let's cite some verses for concept:

> *Ephesians 5:22-26 For wives, this means submit to your husbands as to the Lord. (23) For a husband is the head of his wife as Christ is the head of the church. He is the Savior of his body, the church. (24) As the church submits to Christ, so you wives should submit to your husbands in everything. (25) For husbands, this means love your wives, just as Christ loved the church. He gave up his life for her (26) to make her holy and clean, washed by the cleansing of God's word. (NLT)*

Could the context be any clearer? Husband, you are the leader of your home. You are going to have to report to God some day as to your leadership in that home and you will be judged accordingly.

Wives, could your role be any clearer? How has that been working out in your own life? Are you following God's Word or are you following the current culture of this world and taking upon yourself a role that is not given to you by God? You will be much happier and more blessed when you follow God because God set the standard. It was not some male somewhere on earth. To be in a right relationship with your Lord, you must understand and follow what God has given you for your role in the home. Wives, do not usurp your husband's authority and overstep your boundaries. Encourage your husband to take his rightful place. If he does not, ask God what to do.

In Government. One of the three institutions created by God is the Government. In God's Government in the Old Testament, male leadership was always present. Our country does not follow that any longer. There was a time when it did.

Should we have a woman as our leader, such as President or vice president. It does not fit with God's Word. Some will say, "Well, this is our secular government, and it is different." Is it now? What makes it different since God created the institution of Government? If you read Romans 13 you will find that all authority in government comes from God (vs. 1) and they are God's servants. (vs. 4) and I do not think God has changed His will for His institution. Man may change it. People may like it. But is it the will of God for a woman to be placed in authority in Government? No. We should not have a female governor, legislator, senator, or any other leader.

I know this flies in the face of our worldly or should I say our Satanic culture. But we have drifted down the broad road (Mt. 7:13) among many of our Christian women. It has to be sourced in pride. What else could it be?

It is not a put-down for a woman to do God's will and follow godly guidelines. It is called "Holy Living." It is called – Being in the center of God's will! It is putting Christ on the throne of your heart! It is a revolt from the culture of the world!

Why the difference, or is there a difference between the secular and the sacred to the Christian? In Genesis 3:16 we read; Then he said to the woman, *"I will sharpen the pain of your pregnancy and in pain you will give birth. And you will desire to control your husband and he will rule over you."* NLT.

Remember the Garden of Eden. Eve chose not to believe God but to believe a stranger. Her arrogance drove mankind into sin and death and then she led her husband astray. Today, many woman, holding power over their husbands because of loving attraction and the desire to please their mates, arrogantly sway their husbands away from the Scriptures with a Satanic desire for feminism to be the leader and take charge and go away from the eternal principles of Scriptures.

Pastors are afraid to preach on the subject because they are cowards and because we are living in an age of apostasy. They allow women to take leadership positions over men and some even preach in the church pulpit. It is heretical and definitely not Biblical.

There is no difference for the Christian. God is no different. His eternal unchanging principles do not differentiate between when you are in a building you call church, in your home, or in society. He follows the same pattern for the church, the home and the government BECAUSE HE ESTABLISHED ALL THREE. NEVER, NEVER FORGET THAT OR YOU WILL FOREVER BE ON THE WRONG SIDE OF GOD'S WILL FOR YOUR LIFE.

The old revival preacher Dr. Bob Jones Sr. used to say something similar to this: "There is no difference between the secular and the sacred. To the Christian all ground is holy ground and every bush a burning bush." (Quote is as close to what I can remember) In other words, my words, the Biblical commands to the believer function throughout ones movements in society as well as the church. Why would God want us to act and think differently outside of the church? The church is not the building that we meet in, it is composed entirely of born-again people who make up the body and our function remains the same throughout our journeys in societal relationships, including government, home, and worshiping with the body of Christ. There is no difference.

Chapter Two

Twisting the Great Commandment

How do we normally define God when we think of Him? God is love. Right? When we look at I Corinthians 13 we find much about love. I must quote it here and remember, each time the word Charity is used it comes from the Greek word "agape" the word for a special kind of godly "love".

1 Corinthians 13:1-8 Though I speak with the tongues of men and of angels, but have not love, I have become sounding brass or a clanging cymbal. (2) And though I have the gift of prophecy, and understand all mysteries and all knowledge, and though I have all faith, so that I could remove mountains, but have not love, I am nothing. (3) And though I bestow all my goods to feed the poor, and though I give my body to be burned, but have not love, it profits me nothing. (4) Love suffers long and is kind; love does not envy; love does not parade itself, is not puffed up; (5) does not behave rudely, does not seek its own, is not provoked, thinks no evil; (6) does not rejoice in iniquity, but rejoices in the truth; (7) bears all things, believes all things, hopes all things, endures all things. (8) Love never fails. But whether there are prophecies, they will fail;

whether there are tongues, they will cease; whether there is knowledge, it will vanish away.

In another passage, Jesus was being tested by a lawyer of the Pharisees who asked Him...

Matthew 22:36-40 Master, *which is the great commandment in the law? (37) Jesus said unto him, Thou shalt love the Lord thy God with all thy heart, and with all thy soul, and with all thy mind. (38) This is the first and great commandment. (39) And the second is like unto it, Thou shalt love thy neighbor as thyself. (40) On these two commandments hang all the law and the prophets.*

All throughout the New Testament we are encouraged and commanded to love others. John says that if we hate (do not love) our brother, it is evidence or fruit of an unbeliever (I John 2:9).

Now that seems quite harsh. Many Christians express hatred. Many times, it is for other Christians in the church or people they work with. Neither are acceptable to God. Love is designed to conquer those feelings if we are staying in a close relationship with God.

So, when we talk about the Road to Apostasy or Wallowing in the Mire in the New Testament Church, we do not have to look very far for evidence of it. The evidence is quite visible.

CLUE FOUR: Emphasis On Love While Compromising On Sin.

One of the greatest flaws in Churches today is this issue of using love as a means of an acceptance of sinful behaviors.

Much of the time it begins in the home and then extends into society. First of all, parents who allow their children to be involved in sinful activities leads to the acceptance of sinful behaviors in society.

Why do parents fall into this trap of Satan? It is for two reasons. One: they are tired of fighting with their children, so they give up and compromise. Two: some parent's want their children to be popular with the unsaved children so they allow the kids to participate in activities that are normally not attended by children from godly homes.

I have watched these scenarios play out over many years. My own parents held the line without giving in to those temptations. Also, I wanted to serve God with my life. Thus, I did not participate in what was considered ungodly activities and abstained. I have also watched as parents fought, mainly with girls, who wanted to be involved in activities that Christians normally did not partake in, until finally the parents gave in and let them participate. I have also observed a number of Christian teens who would sneak off to ungodly activities without their parent's knowledge and participated wholeheartedly in them.

On the other hand, I have watched as some parents have pushed their children to participate in questionable activities so they could be with the popular kids at school so they would not be left out or be thought of as strange Christian kids who were weird.

In our society today, many Christians have had to deal with pressures of gender confusion and outlandish behaviors as well as music that does not lend itself well to a Christian lifestyle. Subjects taught in our schools today are far from being based on Christian morality.

My question is, do we want to live for Christ or for self? Are we willing to take up our cross and follow Him or not? Where do we really stand when it comes to our relationship with Christ? I think you will find that those who want to follow the world and the culture are not genuinely born-again believers. If there is no evidence of a person wanting to serve Christ then there is no seed that sprouted in the heart, because it fell on dry hard ground and died.

In revival meetings I preached a message titled "Seven Danger Signals of a False Profession." I was always amazed at the number of church members who came forward week after week to confess they needed to be saved. Deacons, schoolteachers, teens and all ages came forward to commit their lives to Christ or to make sure of it. I believe it is better to be sure than to have questions and I believe many people sitting in our pews are not saved. Thus we see the extent to which worldly living exists in our churches today and the obvious downward slide into apostasy stemming from undisciplined Christians sowing wild oats. Remember, what you sow you will also reap!

It is not surprising to see people compromising on sin under the banner of love. People will say that we must love and accept all kinds of immoral people into our churches. My question is, where do we draw the line? If a person is LGBTQ, we would certainly love them in Christ but would not be accepting of their lifestyle, however, that is what some people are teaching or living. I would not attend a same-sex wedding even if it was a family member. That would be a compromise with sinfulness. If preaching were Biblical, that is, preaching the whole counsel of God, those involved in a homosexual lifestyle or adulterous relationships would either stop listening or cease coming to the services.

If it was a church member, we would follow Scriptural teaching and confront them in love. If they repent, we have won a brother or sister. After three times, we would put them out of membership in the church, that is, if they are a member. If not a member, they would be free to attend, should they desire to learn more of God's Word.

Love does not give us the option to compromise on sin. Period. No matter the situation.

You may think that an attitude is not loving if one seeks to stand for holiness and righteousness. But, one should do it because they love a person, not because one wants to hit them over the proverbial head with a Bible. Being unkind is breaking God's commands.

My wife gives this illustration. If a mother has children and she tells those children not to play in the street and she finds them playing in the street. What does she do? She instructs them again. The second time this happens she instructs them not to play in the street with more energy to get across the danger of that behavior. The third time she finds them she tans their little hide to help convince them of the danger. Why? Because she likes to? No! Because she loves them very much and does not want anything tragic to happen to them.

It is the same with God. He chastens those He loves. If He does not chasten you, you are not one of His. (Hebrews 12:5-8)

Love does not condone sinful behavior. It chastens it with love. It is not accepting of it because sinful activities are never acceptable, no matter who it is or what it is. Immoral behavior is not pleasing to God and we should never make excuses for its acceptance. We must stick to the Word, and in love teach our children and with friendships, we must never seem accepting.

Chapter Three

Subverting God's Teaching On Justice

God says a lot about justice in the Scriptures. Our laws in the United States are based much on what God has to say about justice. In the Great Commandment He sums it up in to "love our neighbor as ourselves." That means to do no harm to our neighbor, to help him as you have the ability to help him, to not steal from him, and to do what you can if he needs food and clothing or medical help along with other things. We are to help the poor as best we can with what God enables us the ability to do.

We see that narrative in the parable of The Good Samaritan. A good lesson for us all. We are not to just pass by someone in need of help, but we are to take the time to help that person.

There are many Scriptures about God's justice that I would like to quote here to refresh our memory.

Psalm 89:14 Justice and judgment are the habitation of thy throne: mercy and truth shall go before thy face.

Solomon speaking on The Beginning of Knowledge says: *Proverbs 1:3 To receive the instruction of wisdom, justice, and judgment, and equity;*

Speaking of Jesus: *Isaiah 9:7 Of the increase of his government and peace there shall be no end, upon the throne of David, and upon his kingdom, to order it, and to establish it with judgment and with justice from henceforth even for ever. The zeal of the LORD of hosts will perform this.*

Jeremiah 23:5 Behold, the days come, saith the LORD, that I will raise unto David a righteous Branch, and a King shall reign and prosper, and shall execute judgment and justice in the earth.

Luke 18:7 And will not God surely see to it that justice is done to his chosen ones who cry out to him day and night, and will he delay toward them? LEB

(Notation, the KJV does not have "justice" inserted in the New Testament even though the sense of the passage and the Greek word would infer it, thus I used the LEB which is a very literal translation for Luke 18:7. I wanted you to see that "justice is used in the NT.)

Justice and Righteousness. In the Scriptures, these go together like two peas in a pod. They are connected with each other. You cannot have one without the other.

I am not going to go into a long dissertation on the subject, but I want to be clear about how Biblical justice is being distorted today by those who twist the truth.

You cannot have justice without righteousness. And you cannot be righteous without being just. They cannot be separated. True justice is righteous. Thus, the false narrative in our society today is by preachers who misuse the Bible's teachings and pervert its meaning on what true justice is. That brings me to our next clue.

CLUE FIVE: Emphasis on Social Justice – Not the Gospel

O, how we see the churches tumble from their Biblical calling. They go down a path from winning people to Christ to triumphing social issues from their pulpits. Many of these preachers, in my opinion, have never met the Savior, that is, never were born again, thus they do not preach the true Gospel of our Lord Jesus Christ.

They want us to welcome the immoral and the deviant in our society, the destructive elements that would tear down our cities as well as our churches. They tell us not to judge – the favorite phrase lost people use against Christian morality! Rather than seeking folk to present the Gospel to that can change their life, many in the church today would have us accepting of their sin, approving their behaviors as if these were okay with God.

Social justice does not change the heart. It just makes dependent people out of those seeking help. Yes, we can help people as God leads, and we should. But the Scriptures deal with heart issues and the teaching for the church is to help other members of the church and care for their needs. You will be hard pressed to find where Scripture tells us to go into all the world and feed and clothe the world. Or stress racial issues because there is no "race" in Scripture but the human race. Dwelling on political issues is not God's way. We know that out of the heart a man speaks and chooses his way in the world. We must deal with heart issues. Only God can change a man's heart, thus amending his way toward others in this world. You cannot legislate righteousness.

The church is not to be teaching its people to do community work as if it were specified in the Bible. That is what the liberal churches do because they have no truth and do not follow the Gospel. Instead, they teach politics and performing community tasks to salve their dislike of the truth of the Gospel, which is, going into all the world and making disciples as people commit their lives to Jesus. The church is to teach its people to share the gospel with others. Today, we are teaching a social gospel and preaching social justice which is not what we are called to do.

Years ago, when liberal leaning churches sent missionaries to foreign lands, they would teach people how to farm the land but did not give them the Gospel that Jesus is the only way to salvation. That is wrong. It does not obey The Great Commission at all.

Today, they teach about helping the homeless, giving out food, serving in soup kitchens, and helping the community. That is all well and good, but so much of it is one without the task of presenting the gospel to them. Spiritual needs are the emphasis in Scripture, not physical needs. It is fine to give a homeless person some money or food, but most important is sharing salvation through Jesus. That is our mission in life and that is being neglected. It makes people feel good to serve physical needs but that is not the mission of the church. The church's purpose is redemption, that is, the gospel on the move throughout the world.

One of the problems seen in the area of social justice is preaching about such issues in the church or from the pulpit. Many a good preacher has fallen from preaching the Gospel to ranting about social justice. God did not call the church to preach such things, but to preach the Word, the Gospel of Jesus Christ.

Hatred will always be with us in our communities. Preaching without the end-product being changed lives is useless. You cannot change people without the Gospel that transforms the heart.

Preachers must do their duty and preach the Word. Everyone understands and can see the tension caused by hatred, but that will not change the heart and you cannot change a person without the Gospel and repentance. True believers love others and love is from God. I have never known a genuine Christian to hate someone just because of the color of their skin. By the way, Martin Luther King was a modernist preacher. He believed that The Millennial Kingdom of God was going to come about because we humans would make the world ready (think righteous enough) for Jesus to come and reign in that kingdom. That is a very telling and consequently a false view of Christ's Millennial Kingdom to come. That is what the churches teach today that do not think that Christ's deity matters, nor that the Virgin Birth is important, nor that we receive Grace (salvation) through trusting Christ by only faith (not works) in our Savior, nor that Jesus died as our substitutionary atonement on the cross, nor that the Bible is the inspired Word of God. I am speaking about the United Methodist, most of the Presbyterians, Catholics, and many others. It comes from people and denominations that do not believe in the fundamental facts of the Scripture as important. These churches promote women preachers and some, gay preachers, gay marriage, false teachings, and mock those who still believe God's Word is The Truth.

God help us to stay on the path of truth, God's truth!

PART II

The Churches Slide Into Compromise

There are several reasons that the church has drifted into compromise. Culture, conflict, worldliness, desiring to please man instead of God, to be accepted in the world, sin, lack of faith in God's Word though preached often, and many others. We will look at these traits in greater detail in the following segments.

Chapter Four

The Christian School Domino Effect

Most of this downward spiral begins with the schooling of pastors and Christian workers. If you look at the Christian colleges and universities today you will see a mix of liberal theology and theistic evolution taught.

Parents send their children off to these schools thinking that their young minds are going to be taught the Word of God in truth, but the schools are more interested in drawing enough students in order to make enough money to make ends meet. Thus, the compromises with a fallen world. It is sad and disgraceful to our Lord and Savior.

For example, Palm Beach Atlantic University in 2020 invited a popular fellow who writes The Babylonian Bee to speak in their chapel. Students protested and there was such an uproar because this fellow had written about the LGBTQ crowd and BLM as being a terrorist group that they uninvited him. He was a graduate from that school and had recently donated $300,000 to help their Masters program. Such disingenuous

Christianity that denies Biblical teachings runs rampant in our so-called Christian schools.

Wheaton College had been known for its great Christian influence over the years. However, when I was in university, back in the 60s their college was teaching theistic evolution instead of teaching Genesis one as authentic. Many Christian schools have caved into liberal theology. Thus our churches have become more liberal in morality and Biblical theology. It all goes together, and it has been going on for many years. Once you begin to deny parts of God's Word and become your own judge, you make up your own definitions for morality and begin the slide downward to compromise Scripture.

Many of the Christian schools and seminaries have turned to more progressive theology and adopted a more liberal teaching. Fuller Theological Seminary was begun years ago. Their namesake and founder was Charles E Fuller, a great preacher that leaned toward fundamentalism and dispensational teachings. He had a radio program called "Old Fashioned Revival Hour. My father would listen to him on the radio when I was a kid and I heard much of his preaching. He would turn over in his grave if he knew where his seminary was theologically today. The former president of Fuller was leading a group called "Evangelicals for Biden." Not a great testimony for a Christian today, but Fuller has been going downhill theologically for many years, sliding from a conservative viewpoint to a more liberal view.

In the past, Fuller had Carl F H Henry as its leader. He was very much an intellectual. He wrote a little booklet called "The Uneasy Conscience of Modern Fundamentalism." It, in my opinion, championed the idea of social justice. It was a downward trend in Fuller Seminary's demise into modern liberalism. Students were being led into social activism. If you wonder why many in the younger generation champion social causes take note of the educational system, secular and Christian.

As the seminaries go, so goes the churches. You used to be able to trust many of the Bible schools but today, you had better check their beliefs because so many have forfeited a conservative and fundamental belief in the foundational doctrines of Scriptures.

CLUE SIX: Little Preaching on Repentance

John the Baptist, the forerunner of Christ, preached repentance. Repentance means changing your ways and the direction that you were going, sort of doing an about-face. It means to change from sin and sinful ways and seek to walk and live more like Christ. It carries the idea of regret, that is, regretting your sinning against God and thus allowing Christ to help you change your sinful attitudes and living.

In churches today, we see very little of people with changed lives. So many live in the world and of the world. So there is little difference between what the world does and what the Christian does. Jesus said we were in the world but not of the world. Meaning that we did not follow the sinful ways of the world in which we live. We are to be different, which means we are to be separated from an unholy lifestyle.

Jesus said the world would hate Christians because they hated Him. So when we are living for Christ, we will not be close friends with the sinful world. We will not act like them, or dress like them if that dress shadows the worlds immorality. So many "so-called" Christians look, act, live, and are molded in the sinful worlds' image and not in Christ's image.

The sinful world hates the holiness of God. You have to tone down your holy living to be accepted by the world and that has happened to Christians and to Churches. The world does not like a genuine Christian for very long. When they find that you do not accept their ways, they get uncomfortable and do not want to be very close to you. It is similar to the analogy that oil and water do not mix and cannot mix. They are separate substances and repel each other. Christians will love the lost person, but the lost person will not want to be your best friend unless he or she comes to a knowledge of Christ and follows Him.

I could list many ways that a Christian is disliked by the world, but I will only give a few. Christians that follow Christ and read their Bibles regularly do not believe in killing babies in the womb or out of the womb. The world's evolutionary view is that it does not matter because they are just a blob of flesh. Get rid of it if you do not want that child. To the Christian, each baby is formed in the womb by God and is a precious child coming into existence. Genuine believers in Christ do not believe that homosexuality, same sex marriages, and transgenderism is holy, because it defies God's ordained holiness in intimacy as He created it to be for the purpose of producing children and growing a family to honor Him.

In America today, many churches have given in to the world's idea of sexuality. They no longer stand with God's word, but compromise to the world's standards. There are gay and lesbian folk taking on the form of preachers and ministers. They marry same-sex couples. All of that kind of church is repulsive to God Almighty and the Lord Jesus Christ because it is forbidden by Scripture.

Thus, many churches have quit preaching on repentance. They only talk about the love of God and eliminate preaching on sin and wrong living. It might cause their churches to be smaller and the offerings to be down. They do not want conflict but they do have a love for money and big buildings, so they water down the Gospel of Christ. It has been the cause of Christian complacency in the pews. Thus our churches are full of unrepentant people who are not saved and also are full of many Christians who live in friendship with the world's ungodly ways.

CLUE SEVEN: An Emphasis on Money

The average church is deeply concerned with emphasizing money. Television preachers preach the prosperity gospel. Churches build multi-million-dollar buildings. Preachers emphasize the tithe, faith promise giving, missionary funding, freewill offerings, and legacy giving along with fund-raisers etc. Otherwise, they would collapse and die.

Now, I believe in giving to the Lord's work, much like Paul taught. But you will never find Paul raising money to build large edifices called church buildings. Paul never taught on the tithe. Paul raised money for some widows and orphans in Jerusalem. Paul taught us to give cheerfully, not of necessity because God loves a cheerful giver.

Preachers twist the Word of God on money. It is sad. God's Word says that the love of money is the root of evil. Thus, it has been used and abused by many, otherwise good preachers as well as many evil preachers.

Many preachers teach people to tithe. I will not go into a long teaching on this subject but suffice it to say that modern churches rely on the tithe to pay for their buildings and staff. They use the Old Testament theocratic rule to raise money to keep things afloat. Never once did the Apostle Paul teach on it. Why? Because it was for another time and purpose. It was not carried on to the church because the whole situation changed from the Israelites theocratic commands. It was basically a Temple tax and there were several tithes in the Old Testament -Not just one type of tithe.

Many times, I've wondered if God wanted us to build big buildings to worship in. My thinking is that we copied the Catholic Church in its buildings, type of worship and style of having church. Much of that came from out of the Reformation by people and preachers who had been associated with the Catholic Church. The true church which began in the New Testament has functioned throughout the centuries outside of the Catholic

Church. It was the evangelicals who came out of the Reformation that had a big influence on church services. The evangelicals are the Presbyterians, Methodists, Congregational churches, and others that sprang from those such as the Holiness groups, Pentecostals, Wesleyans, Four Square, and others. Those who functioned before the Reformation were the Baptists, Anti-Baptists and other groups that were constantly opposed by the Catholic Church (who persecuted and killed many believers) because they were anti-infant baptism. Thus, I am not an evangelical because I hold to Baptist theology and teachings, not Reformed nor Calvinism. There were also those who called themselves Reformed Baptists being inspired by the freedom brought about by the Reformation.

We have spent much of God's money on large buildings. I think our idea of church is so skewed today, we just follow what others are doing without perhaps, knowing or understanding truly what God desires. The churches in the New Testament met mostly in homes and perhaps other buildings. I am not opposed to having or meeting in a building that is larger than a home. I just think we have overspent on large buildings that sit empty most of the week.

CLUE EIGHT: Not Believing Genesis One

Most nights my wife and I listen to books on *audible* or *Chirp*, mainly Christian themed books. One afternoon I received a new book that I was excited to listen to by a scholar Dennis Prager called *The Rational Bible* and the subject was a commentary on Genesis.[2]

After a few nights listening to the introduction and then the first few verses on Genesis, I returned the book and opted for another. It made me sick listening to him parrot the theme of lost scholars and supposed theologians. He stated there were fifteen billion years before Genesis one that looked backward and that Genesis one looked forward.

It was the fifteen billion years that hit me in the stomach. That is the theme of theistic evolutionists and the worlds' godless atheists who teach evolution as a fact. Dr. Prager went on to discuss how he had a lot of friends that believed in a young earth who were very sincere and good people but wrong.

As for me, I just take Genesis chapter one as it is written and it makes perfect sense. The word "Day" in Hebrew can mean periods of time just as we use the term today, but its actual meaning is a 24-hour period. The Scripture states, evening and morning were the first day. That is about as clear as one can get.

What convinced me of seven literal days of creation was in Exodus 20:9-11 in the neighborhood of The Ten Commandments:

Exodus 20:9 Six days shalt thou labor, and do all thy work:

Exodus 20:10 But the seventh day is the sabbath of the LORD thy God: in it thou shalt not do any work, thou, nor thy son, nor thy daughter, thy manservant, nor thy maidservant, nor thy cattle, nor thy stranger that is within thy gates:

Exodus 20:11 For in six days the LORD made heaven and earth, the sea, and all that in them is, and rested the seventh day: wherefore the LORD blessed the sabbath day, and hallowed it.

Is anything **more** clear than that!?!!! It is obvious that God only used six days to create the world, not billions of "who knows how many" years! There is no gap noted. It is only men who want to cast doubt on the Word of God and compromise with the atheistic so-called scientists who promote such false teachings. This also makes it possible to doubt other passages so that one can decide for himself which passages are truth and which are not. Red flags are abundant!

Explaining away a crucial passage like Genesis is simply a way to compromise with Satan's world. A believer accepts the Scripture by faith even when he cannot understand some portions and accepts it at face value. A simple reading of Genesis one is not hard to understand what God did.

PART III

The Road Upward – Returning to Righteousness in Your Church

Things must change if you are going to kick the world out of your church body or the downward spiral will continue. Pastors must give an answer to God for their leadership in that "called out group" of believers. Is your reward the wood, hay, and stubble of a worldly church or will it go through the fire and the refinement will be pure gold. It's your call. No one else will answer for your leading the sheep. It is a sobering thought.

What has been your goal? To bring in more people by lowering the standards of righteousness and allowing the culture of this world to permeate your group? Is that how you think? More people makes the church look more successful and perhaps brings in more funds.

Are you willing to compromise in order to have bigger crowds? I trust not! We need some Samuel's who do not seek to curry favor with those who handle the purse strings.

PART III: The Road Upward – Returning to Righteousness in Your Church

RESTORE POINT 1: Repentance – as a church or an individual, renew your relationship with God.

Repentance involves a change of mind that causes one to change his direction. One must determine in his heart that he will not defile himself with the sinful culture of this world. It is a heart issue.

When we read the story of Daniel in the Old Testament, do you not admire him in his determined stance for the glory of God? Are we not proud of him as a young man in a pagan country standing true to his commitment to God's commandments? Of course we do as we all love to read his story in God's Word.

What about the courage of Shadrach, Meshach, and Abednego and the fiery furnace? Big and powerful Nebuchadnezzar ask them *"Is it true…do you not serve my gods, nor worship the golden image which I have set up?"* The trio answers *"We will not serve your gods nor worship your image."* We all would have been shaking in our boots with our knees knocking.

Then these pagans, following the instructions of their king, stoked up the fire seven times. Basically they were saying "We'll show you whose is boss!" But that did not deter the young men from serving God. The fire was so hot that the guards that threw them in died on the spot from the heat. But, did the young men die? No! They were not afraid of standing true to God, even if it meant they would have to give up their lives. Nebuchadnezzar looked and said *"I see four men loose, walking in the midst of the fire…and the fourth is like the Son of God."*

My question is: How weak are we as Christians in this modern environment of disobedience to God? Are we shaking in our boots at the criticism of this world? Why should we be frightened? Is our God too weak to protect us? Do we really believe that He is more powerful than these earthly people who defy His Name? Is our weakness showing? We have much to repent concerning our confidence in God Almighty!

As a church, we need to publicly repent as a congregation for our lack of determination to keep sinful worldliness out of the church so that we may honor our Lord with our desire to worship in His righteousness.

RESTORE POINT 2: Righteousness – put on the new man and walk in holiness.

Are you afraid of a holy church? Will it cramp your style and make you look out of touch with those around you in your community? Or do you want to be in touch with God, walking in holiness while people outside the church turn up their nose at your holy practices and think of you as too prudish and out of date? These are questions we have to answer and perhaps more quickly than we are prepared to do.

What has happened to holiness in the church? Has it been abandoned? Notice what Paul says in Ephesians 4:24 *"And that you put on the new man, which after God is created in righteousness and true holiness."*

The church (which Biblically means the people, not the building) must follow God in holiness by becoming holy in word, deed, and heart. That is our godly destination. We may never get to the end in this life but we are to travel that direction. It means becoming holy in our outward life as well as our inward heart. God judges us on the intent of the heart, not on our outward appearances. However, the inward determination of the heart is usually apparent in our outward walk.

I believe that is what Paul meant in Philippians 2:12 *Wherefore, my beloved, as ye have always obeyed, not as in my presence only, but now much more in my absence, work out your own salvation with fear and trembling.* God puts it in us and we are to work it out. He imputes righteousness and holiness into us and we must work it out in living and walking outwardly in holiness.

In God's commandments to Aaron and his sons in Leviticus10:10 He states this important message: *You must distinguish between the holy and the common, and the clean and the unclean,"* (HCSB) We too must learn to distinguish between holy and sinful.

I believe we have failed in our church meetings, in music, in preaching and teaching concerning holiness. We have bent the teachings from Scripture to conform to this world so we would seem more affable and pleasant to this sinful and unholy world in which we live. We are fearful of losing members so we skip certain passages such as holiness in living or we water it down. We have not followed the Scriptures when it comes to our music. So much of our services allow women to lead which is inappropriate Scripturally. We water down holy living. We bend the meaning of Scripture so as not to anger certain people. We have compromised truth!

The Church needs to repent and renew its calling and conform to Scripture above all else and to stand boldly for holiness and righteousness. It is imperative and urgent for us to change our unacceptable practices in order to be in a right standing with God Almighty.

RESTORE POINT 3: Prune - getting rid of dead sinful and unholy branches in your church body and practices.

It is time to make some important changes for righteousness. It may be time for some church discipline. Getting rid of a rock band approach in a worship setting. Getting rid of preaching comprising sermons and preach The Word in Truth, Power, and thoroughly, not leaving out the difficult parts that might upset some folk.

Are you more comfortable in a relationship with the world than preaching the Truth of the Word. My question to you is: "Who called you? The world or God?" It's time to preach truth to a lost world and stop being a pansy which in essence means a tool of the devil!

Stop being mindful of money or salary and be mindful of what God has given us to do. Change worldly practices that are eating away your testimony and watch what God can and will do through a determined effort to rid your church of unrighteousness. Be a leader preacher and quit compromising in order to be liked or acceptable to a fallen world.

It is not you that brings people to saving faith in God! It is the Holy Spirit Who convicts and leads people to repentance. Quit worrying about programs and practices and get on your knees. Prayer is our communication with the God of this universe and He is the One Who brings blessing and success in our churches. Quit relying on worldly ways to achieve growth. Believe wholly in that Bible that you teach and preach and follow God's way. If you fail to achieve numbers, you fail. Your success is not what God is after. He is looking for faithful men and women to do His will. People who want His leadership. People who want His Name to be honored and not their own.

It is time to prune those dead branches of man's achievements and successes. Get rid of man's interference in God's work. Let God be God and trust him rather than relying on your own philosophies which are dead weight. Go forward and stop hampering God's doing.

Stop creating and scheduling so many programs that cause people to be at the church building so often. People do not need to be running all the time so one looks successful. They need time to meditate on God's Word and prayer in the privacy of their own homes. Busyness is not godly nor spiritual. It is difficult enough just going to work, taking care of family and chores at home while seeking time to be alone with God. Prune off those needless things in ones schedule.

Pruning helps a tree to grow and flourish. It allows the life giving nourishment to reach to the end of the branches to make them healthy rather than to dead branches that sap its strength. The application to the church is appropriate. We have too much dead wood that hinders the Spirit of God's working in our church. If you do not believe that is so, remember Jesus was limited by the unbelief of people in his home town.

Why is that so? Because God works through our lives to reach this world. Yes, He could just say the Word and all would be well but God chose to work through His children to reach a lost world.

Prune the dead and sick branches from your church. Help it to have the freedom to grow better and become more healthy spiritually. If you question this principle, go back and read John 15.

RESTORE POINT 4: Salt and Light - you should be an irritant as well as light in your community!

When you live and walk with Jesus, you will not only light up the pathway for some people, but you will irritate others who do not share your choice of righteousness. It takes courage and a commitment to honor Jesus Christ.

We are to walk in love but that love carries with it hatred from this world. It causes Satan to be angry and seek to destroy you along with your testimony. Are you prepared for that?

Standing up with Jesus and for Jesus is an irritant to a worldly culture. They will not like you and they will not want to be around you. It causes them friction. They will hate what you stand for but that is what bearing your cross is all about.

Many have been martyred simply because they are believers in Christ. In India, the middle east, in China, in Africa and around the world, people are being persecuted and killed because they name the Name of Christ Jesus. In America, we have not suffered that kind of persecution yet, but it is coming soon.

One would think that by living for God, loving your neighbor, walking in holiness that one would be respected. However, such is not the case. Jesus told us that in this world we would have persecution but we did not think He was referring to us. That must be meant for others in other parts of the world. Just keep your eyes open because it is beginning to happen in the good old USA. Actually, it is already happening fiercely.

Determine and understand that you are salt and light. Salt preserves and cleanses, purifies and irritates. Light shines brightly and most people appreciate that, however God's Word warns us that men love darkness rather than light because their deeds are evil. You see, along with the joys, there are sorrows. Along with the good comes evil and evil is vicious and deadly. Are you prepared? Your protection comes from the Lord and the Armour of God.

We must be ready and prepared for battle spiritually. We cannot be cowardly. God gives us boldness to face evil and light to cancel darkness that seeks to stop us. However, we are to put on the armor of God because you cannot stand up or survive in a fallen world ruled by Satan without it. Let's be salt and light without apology! Let's quit making excuses for our weakness and remember that nothing can separate us from the love of God.

I leave you with this passage which I love dearly:

Romans 8:34-39

(35) Who shall separate us from the love of Christ? shall tribulation, or distress, or persecution, or famine, or nakedness, or peril, or sword?

(36) As it is written, For thy sake we are killed all the day long; we are accounted as sheep for the slaughter.

(37) Nay, in all these things we are more than conquerors through him that loved us.

(38) For I am persuaded, that neither death, nor life, nor angels, nor principalities, nor powers, nor things present, nor things to come,

(39) Nor height, nor depth, nor any other creature, shall be able to separate us from the love of God, which is in Christ Jesus our Lord.

Epilogue/Conclusion

I have sought to lay out some principles to help guide and inspire the Church of Jesus Christ. Please prayerfully consider these steps to help yourself and your local assembly. This book has been on my heart for several years now. I began writing its pages but then I thought to myself, "Why?" Who am I to seek to teach and instruct others. I am nothing in the Christian world of today. There are much more scholarly and intelligent men of God than I. However, the Holy Spirit kept impressing upon me to finish this book. So that is what I did.

I tried to keep it short and concise so one could read and digest it in a couple of hours instead of several days because the appointed time is near. I thought, Jesus will come before I finish this small book and I will have failed to publish in time. So, thank God, His coming tarried long enough.

That being said, I long for His return and He cannot come too quickly for me. I want to see Him. As the old hymn says, "I want to see my Savior first of all. Before on any others I would call. And then for countless days… on His dear face I'll gaze. I want to see my Savior first of all."

There are many I want to see. My son who went to be with our Lord when he was so young and beautiful. I have longed to see and be with him since the accident. I want to see him, hug him and tell him how much I missed him. My parents I want to see and many others like David, and Daniel, Paul and John, but I want to see my Savior first of all.

Bibliography

KJV - Scripture quotations from The Authorized (King James) Version. Rights in the Authorized Version in the United Kingdom are vested in the Crown. Reproduced by permission of the Crown's patentee, Cambridge University Press

HCSB - Holman Christian Standard Bible. Scripture quotations marked HCSB have been taken from the Holman Christian Standard Bible, Copyright 1999, 2000, 2002, 2003, 2009 by Holman Bible Publishers. Used by permission. Holman Christian Standard Bible, Holman CSB, and HCSB are federally registered trademarks of Holman Bible Publishers.

LEB - Scripture quotations marked (LEB) are from the Lexham English Bible. Copyright 2012 Logos Bible Software. Lexham is a registered trademark of Logos Bible Software.

NLT - Scripture quotations marked (NLT) are taken from the Holy Bible, New Living Translation, copyright © 1996, 2004, 2015 by Tyndale House Foundation. Used by permission of Tyndale House Publishers, Carol Stream, Illinois 60188, USA. All rights reserved.

References

1. Biden, Joe AP: "*I will flat out just change the law. Every — eliminate those executive orders, number one.*" "*The idea that an 8-year-old child or a 10-year-old child decides, 'You know I decided I want to be transgender. That's what I think I'd like to be. It would make my life a lot easier.' There should be zero discrimination.*" (October 21, 2020 AP)
2. *The Rational Bible: Genesis*, Dennis Prager, *Audible*, May 2019
3. Albert Barnes' Notes on the Bible from e-Sword LT

Acknowledgments

I had the privilege of living in a chalet between the late Evangelist Del Fehsenfeld and the late Dr. Ed Hindson overlooking Clear Lake in Michigan. I was a young preacher in my early 30's and we did revival meetings for Life Action Crusades. It was the early 70's. I owe so much to both of these men. They both were great men of God.

I learned much from Del about doing revivals and about what kind of preaching and prayer was necessary to help awaken churches to revival.

The late Dr. Ed Hindson was like an encyclopedia of Biblical knowledge. He preached much on prophecy and I loved listening when he spoke.

I admired them both very much and I cannot express my gratitude enough for what I learned from both of these great men of God.

I also owe much to two of my professors at Bob Jones University, the late Mr. Clemens and the late Dr. Fred Afman, Mr. Clemens taught Teachings of Jesus and I learned so much from him. Dr. Afman taught Advanced Old Testament. I learned so much from his class and have used that information throughout the years.

There are many more I could add, but for the sake of being too redundant I decided to list the most influential to my ministry.

About the Author

Dr. Ken Lewis has traveled this great land speaking and ministering in music and teaching since he was fifteen years old. In his home church, he was asked to fill vacation pulpits for various pastors around Kansas from that young age through college.

He felt called to attend Bob Jones University in Greenville, SC where he graduated with a BA in the School of Religion with a Major in Bible and a minor in Speech in 1966. He went on to Tennessee Temple with a year of studies in in Christian Education. Later, he received a Masters in Theology, and went on the get his Doctorate in Theology graduating Summa Cum Laude from Andersonville Theological Seminary.

He traveled across the country singing and preaching while doing Revival Meetings, first on his own, then with Life Action Crusades before beginning his own ministry called Life Dynamics. There he traveled with about 25 – 28 people doing music and revivals. He traveled in revivals with the late Dr. Ed Hindson and the late Del Fehsenfeld as a young 30 year-old preacher. Dr. Ken recorded albums with Life Action Quartet and Life Dynamics. He has preached in over 150 revival meetings, pastored several churches. He also had several radio programs, and did some television shows preaching and various interviews while traveling the country. He basically retired from full-time ministry in 2004.

He has written several booklets and articles especially for revival meetings, a Pastors Manual, and a number of articles for newsletters. He also has had a couple of YouTube channels and a Word Press website where he has written numerous articles.